THIS CANDLEWICK BOOK BELONGS TO:

_____

_____

_____

Cory

Martin

Miguel

Pearl

Mr. Whiskers

Ashley

Willie

Lupita

LARRY

What's the

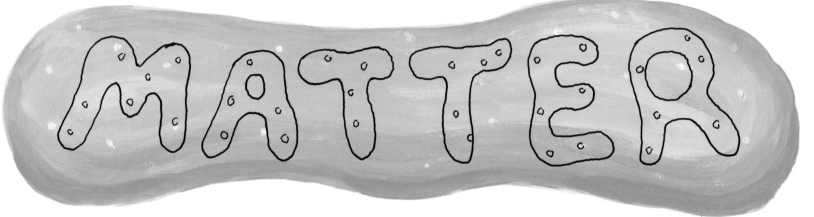

MATTER

in Mr. Whiskers' Room?

Michael Elsohn Ross

illustrated by **Paul Meisel**

CANDLEWICK PRESS

To Samantha from Great Uncle Whiskers
M. E. R.

For Amy and Chris, and my friends at Candlewick
P. M.

Text copyright © 2004 by Michael Elsohn Ross
Illustrations copyright © 2004 by Paul Meisel

First paperback edition 2007

The Library of Congress has cataloged the hardcover edition as follows:
Ross, Michael Elsohn, date.
What's the matter in Mr. Whiskers' Room? / Michael Elsohn Ross ;
illustrated by Paul Meisel. —1st ed.
p.   cm.
ISBN 978-0-7636-1349-5 (hardcover)
1. Science—Experiments—Juvenile literature.
[1. Science—Experiments. 2. Experiments.]
I. Meisel, Paul, ill. II. Title.
Q164.R69 2004
507'.8—dc22   2003069566

ISBN 978-0-7636-3566-4 (paperback)

2 4 6 8 10 9 7 5 3

Printed in China

This book was typeset in Stempel Schneidler and Gill Sans.
The illustrations were done in ink and watercolor.
Colored pencil, gouache, and pastels were also used.

Candlewick Press
99 Dover Street
Somerville, Massachusetts 02144

visit us at www.candlewick.com

A NOTE TO BIG PEOPLE

Kids learn about science by exploring. In my class, I promote open-ended discovery. I watch and listen to the kids at play, and when I think they are ready to consider a big idea, I introduce one, such as "Matter takes up space." All people are born scientists. We are curious and naturally experiment. As adults we can nurture exploration in our children, but we need not meddle in their enthusiastic adventures (unless there is a matter of safety involved).

Mr. Whiskers

One hot Monday in early September, Martin arrived at school with a bellyache. But when he walked into the classroom, he almost forgot all about it.

Mr. Whiskers had a wild look in his eyes, the kind that said something fun was going to happen. There were science kits set up at tables and even outside in the schoolyard. Lots of kids had questions about the kits, but when Mr. Whiskers waved his silence wand, everyone quieted down.

"What's the matter with your stomach, Martin?" whispered Ashley.

"Matter? Did I hear someone say matter?" Mr. Whiskers asked. "That's exactly what we are going to explore today. Matter is stuff, and I have lots of stuff for you to play with."

All the kids wanted to see the stuff, but first Mr. Whiskers pointed out the rules for explorer time.

When he tooted the horn, everyone scattered. Some kids looked at the kits in the classroom, and some checked out the science stations in the schoolyard.

RULES

Start to play when you hear the horn.

Share with other people.

Change groups whenever you wish or when it's too crowded.

Be gentle with things and people.

Have fun.

Help put everything away when I beat the drum.

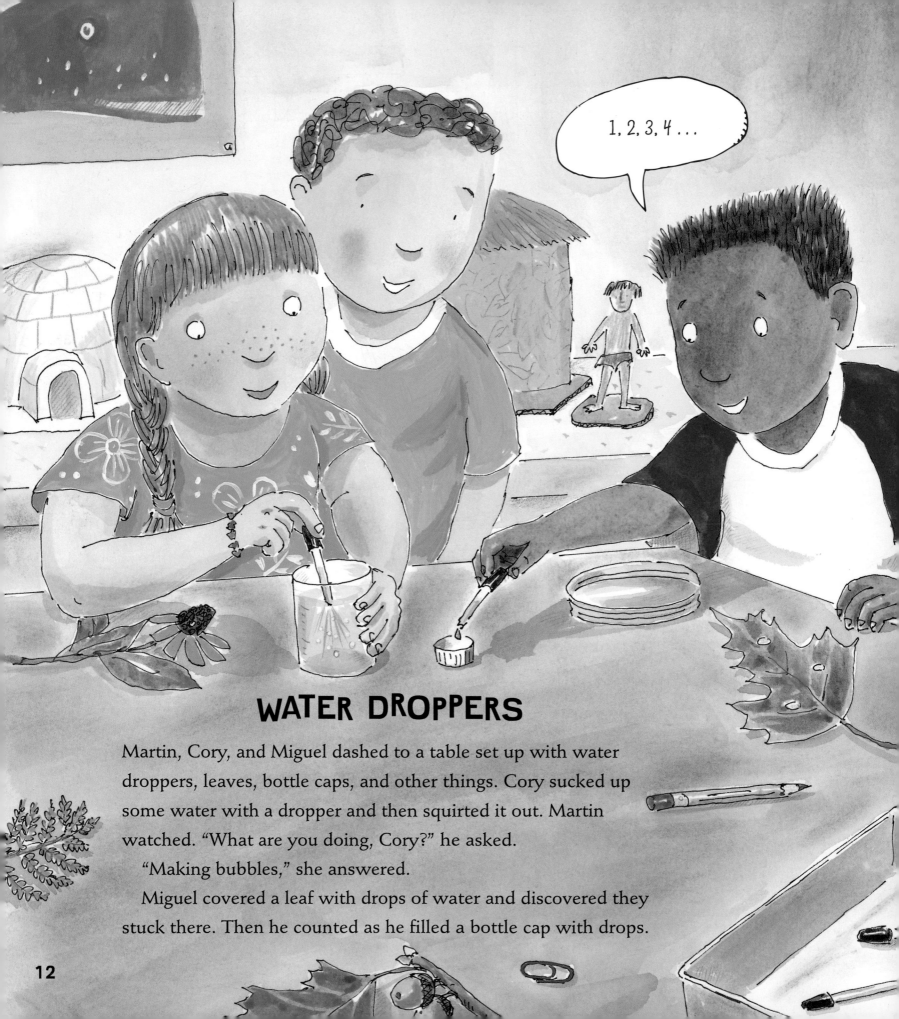

WATER DROPPERS

Martin, Cory, and Miguel dashed to a table set up with water droppers, leaves, bottle caps, and other things. Cory sucked up some water with a dropper and then squirted it out. Martin watched. "What are you doing, Cory?" he asked.

"Making bubbles," she answered.

Miguel covered a leaf with drops of water and discovered they stuck there. Then he counted as he filled a bottle cap with drops.

"Let's do something really fun," Cory announced. She pretended the dropper was a drippy nose. Willie cruised by and looked at Cory but didn't stay to play.

Miguel stuck drops to a pencil, a paper clip, his fingernail, and even to Mr. Whiskers' nose.

"Does water take up space?" Mr. Whiskers asked.

"Water fills up my dropper," said Martin.

Miguel replied, "Drops can fill up a bottle cap."

"Look! Bubbles take up space," Cory announced.

"Toys take up a lot of space in my room," Martin said. "Too much space, my mom says. Hey, maybe everything takes up space."

"That's the big idea," Mr. Whiskers told him. "All matter takes up space!"

I take up space at this table!

15

GLOOP

Martin saw Larry and Ashley over at a table with some interesting blue gloopy stuff. He got there just as Larry grabbed as much of the gloop as he could. "Mine, all mine!" Larry said.

"Larry, you're supposed to share," Ashley reminded him. "Now give some to Martin and me."

Larry frowned but gave a bit to each of the others.

16

Cory came over and took a chunk from Larry too.

"Hey, this feels like rubber," she said.

"It looks like taffy," said Martin.

"It stretches," said Ashley. "Maybe we can add all of ours together and make a snake."

"Maybe we can make candy and eat it," added Martin. "Yum!"

"Martin," Mr. Whiskers called out just as Martin was about to taste some gloop. "Remember, we don't eat any matter during science class, no matter how good it looks."

Ashley said, "Look, Mr. Whiskers. It stretches!"

It's squishy and stretchy and bubbly.

A BIG IDEA!

We can find out about matter by using our senses.

For example, a carrot is matter, and it has a particular taste, smell, color, and shape. Carrots even make a crunchy, snappy sound when you bite into them. We can sense other things too. We can't see air, but we can feel it when the wind blows, and smell the scents that it carries.

"Hmmm," Mr. Whiskers said. "What else did you discover about gloop?"

"Its bubbles make a loud pop!" Cory cried out.

Martin whined, "It looks and smells good enough to eat."

"That's the big idea!" said Mr. Whiskers. "We can find out about matter by using our senses of touch, sight, hearing, and smell. We can also use our sense of taste, but not here, Martin!"

OOBLECK

"Hey, Pearl, what's that stuff?" called Cory as she sat down between Pearl and Miguel at another science station.

They had green slimy stuff dripping from their fingers and squashed between their palms.

"It's oobleck and it changes from hard to soft and back again," Pearl said.

It's slimy like squished bananas.

20

"It's like magic," Miguel said. "It's hard when it's in the dish, but it's drippy when you pick it up."

Martin and Lupita ambled over to the group.

Cory pretended she was sick and cried out, "I'm throwing up green gunk!"

"It's kind of like glue—maybe it would glue your mouth up," Martin said.

"Maybe I can glue my hands together," said Miguel.

It's green and icky!

Mr. Whiskers squeezed some oobleck and let it drip through his fingers. "Do you think this is a liquid, like milk, or a solid, like a cookie?" he asked Cory.

"Sometimes it drips, and sometimes it's solid," she answered.

"It's kind of like a milk shake and kind of like ice cream," added Martin.

I'm getting hungry!

A BIG IDEA!

Matter can come in different forms.

It can be a liquid, a solid, or a gas. Rocks, bones, and trees are solids. Water, lava, and blood are liquids. Helium, propane, and oxygen are gases. What forms of matter can you find around you? Can you locate any gases, liquids, or solids?

"It's hard, but it's gooey," said Pearl.

"I noticed that too," said Mr. Whiskers. "Matter can be a gas, a liquid, or a solid. The fun thing about oobleck is that it changes from a solid to a liquid, then back again."

23

ICE AND WATER

Cory wandered outdoors into the warm sunshine. She spied the blocks of ice that Mrs. Sanchez, the classroom aide, was placing on the blacktop for another science kit. Then Cory set to work inventing an ice-melting machine with mirrors and tinfoil.

"What are you doing, Cory?" Ashley asked.

"I'm going to cook the ice," Cory replied.

Miguel came by and started to write on the blacktop with water and a paintbrush.

"Do you think water will melt the ice?" Ashley asked Cory.

Cory thought for a minute, then said, "I know soda melts ice cubes."

"I sprayed some ice with water, and it melted the ice," Ashley reported.

"My name disappeared from the ground," Miguel added. "Maybe I invented disappearing ink."

Cory asked, "Do you think my ice-melting machine is working?"

When Mr. Whiskers walked by, Miguel called out, "Come and see the disappearing ink."

Mr. Whiskers examined the blacktop and then asked, "Where did the water ink go? Do you think the water changed to something else?"

"I saw steam," Miguel said.

I made ice into water.

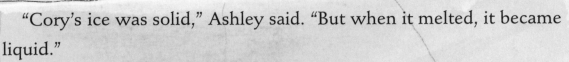

"Cory's ice was solid," Ashley said. "But when it melted, it became liquid."

"Maybe the water changed to steam," Cory added. "It evaporated!"

"That's the big idea!" Mr. Whiskers exclaimed. "Matter can change form—from liquid to solid or gas. The ice changed to water, and the water changed to vapor."

A BIG IDEA!

Matter can change from one form to another.

For instance, ice is solid matter. When it melts, it becomes liquid water. Liquid water can evaporate and become water vapor or steam, which is a gas. Water vapor can condense and become liquid water again. Liquid water can then freeze and become ice. Can *you* make water change form? What other matter can you find that changes form?

27

ROCKS

Ashley went looking for Larry, and found him inside at a table covered with rocks, scales, magnifying lenses, cups of water, tiles, and other things.

She peered at a rock through a magnifying lens and saw sparkles. Larry scraped one rock against another and rubbed his finger over the scratches that he had made. Then he made scratches on other rocks.

Ashley put little rocks on one side of the scale. When she put a big rock on the other side, it sank down.

"Look," she said to Martin, who had wandered over. "This rock is heavier than three little ones."

"This little one looks like a pill," Martin said, and he almost swallowed it but remembered what Mr. Whiskers had said. He dropped it in the water, and it changed color.

Ashley ran over to Mr. Whiskers and pulled him to the table.

"I found the heavyweight rock," she told him.

"Do all rocks have weight?" Mr. Whiskers asked.

"Of course. I think everything has weight," said Ashley.

"If I ate something, I'd have more weight," said Martin.

"If you gave me all the rocks, I'd have a lot of weight," said Larry.

Mr. Whiskers said, "Yes, that's another big idea. All matter has weight!"

I think *my* rock is the heaviest.

A BIG IDEA!
All matter has weight. The more dense an object is, the more it weighs. A pencil is more dense than a straw, so the pencil weighs more than the straw. A book is more dense than a dry sponge of the same size, so the sponge weighs less than the book. What things can you find that are really heavy? What can you find that is light?

WATER TUBS

Larry and Ashley wanted to try something new, so they went outside to do some tests at the water tubs.

"Wow, look at all this stuff!" exclaimed Larry. He grabbed as much as he could. He even tried to take some things that Lupita was using.

"Remember the rules, Larry. You have to share," said Ashley.

Lupita pretended she was giving a toy dinosaur a bath. Willie was hot from wandering all over the place and was cooling off as he poured water through funnels onto one of his hands.

Larry and Ashley found out that an empty bowl floated, but then it sank when they filled it with water. A cork floated, but Lupita's dinosaur sank.

"I wonder what else will float," Ashley said.

"Put the dinosaur in an empty bowl and see what happens," Larry suggested.

The dinosaur rode along inside the floating bowl as if it were in a boat. Willie put a rock in the water and that floated too!

The dinosaur needs a boat to float.

33

34

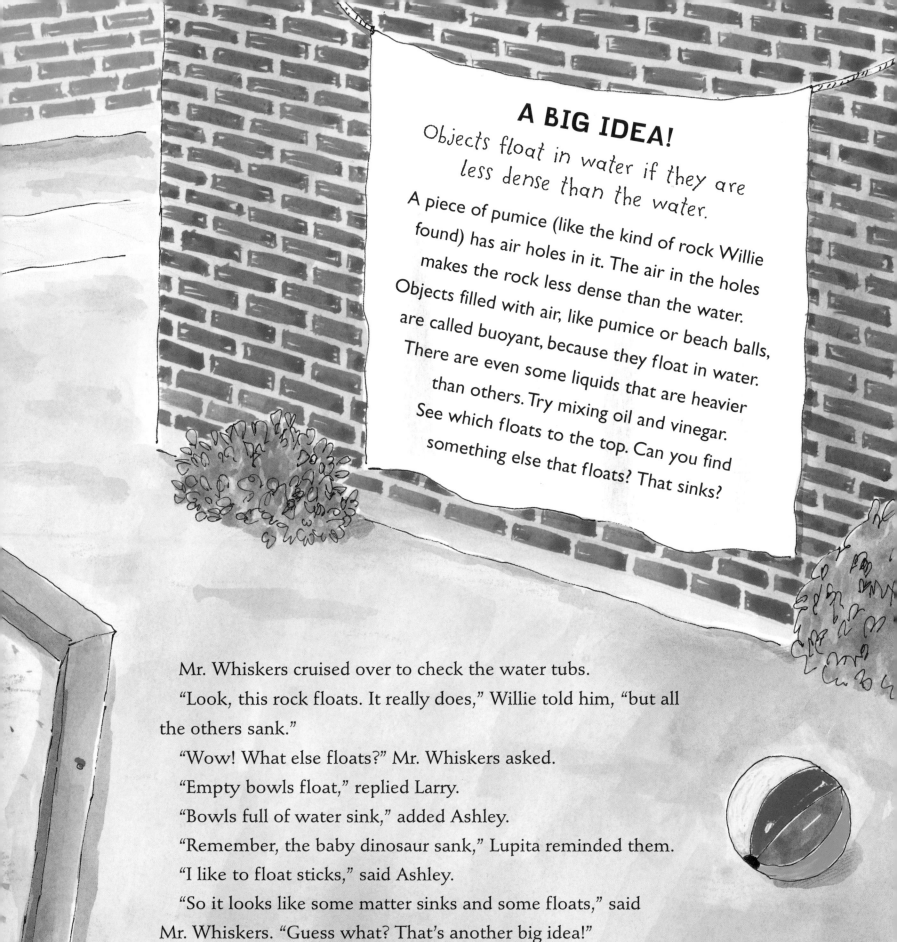

A BIG IDEA!

Objects float in water if they are less dense than the water.

A piece of pumice (like the kind of rock Willie found) has air holes in it. The air in the holes makes the rock less dense than the water. Objects filled with air, like pumice or beach balls, are called buoyant, because they float in water. There are even some liquids that are heavier than others. Try mixing oil and vinegar. See which floats to the top. Can you find something else that floats? That sinks?

Mr. Whiskers cruised over to check the water tubs.

"Look, this rock floats. It really does," Willie told him, "but all the others sank."

"Wow! What else floats?" Mr. Whiskers asked.

"Empty bowls float," replied Larry.

"Bowls full of water sink," added Ashley.

"Remember, the baby dinosaur sank," Lupita reminded them.

"I like to float sticks," said Ashley.

"So it looks like some matter sinks and some floats," said Mr. Whiskers. "Guess what? That's another big idea!"

SAND AND MUD PLAY

Looking for something messier to play with, Cory and Miguel went to the sandbox.

Ashley was there, making cookies from a special recipe of mud, sand, and leaves. Larry was about to take away some of her leaves, but she suggested, "Larry, let's make something together."

"Okay. Let's make a *giant* cookie," said Larry.

They mixed leaves and mud together and made a cookie, but when Larry poured water on it, it turned all mucky.

Larry and Ashley got busy testing new recipes for dirt cookies.
They added more dirt and more water, a little bit at a time.

"Let's make a pretend volcano with dirt," Cory said to Miguel.
"And then we can make some lava by filling the hole on the top of
the volcano with water."

"One, two, three, four, five." Miguel counted the cups of water as
he poured them into the hole. When the hole was full, a river of mud
oozed downhill.

When Mr. Whiskers was nearby, Larry told him, "The water drank up the dirt in our cookie and made it soggy."

"But then we put in some extra dirt, and it drank up the water and made it more solid again," said Ashley. "Look." And she rushed over to show Mr. Whiskers their cookie, but she tripped and it landed on his shoes.

"Oops. Sorry, Mr. Whiskers," apologized Ashley.

"It's only cookie dough," said Mr. Whiskers as he washed it off with water.

"Watch this, Mr. Whiskers," Miguel called out as he poured water into the volcano to make more lava.

"It looks like the water dissolves the dirt when it makes your lava," observed Mr. Whiskers.

"Yeah," replied Miguel, "it sucks it up and carries it away."

"Wow!" said Mr. Whiskers. "It seems like some matter dissolves other matter. What do you know? That's another big idea."

A BIG IDEA!

Some matter dissolves other matter.

Sugar mixes with water to make sugar water. Salt mixes with water to make salt water. Sand doesn't dissolve in water but sinks to the bottom. Dirt will dissolve in water, but after a while it will also sink. Only the tiniest particles of dirt will stay in the water, giving it a dirty color. When a substance dissolves in water, the new substance is called a solution. Can you make some solutions with water and other matter?

The things we know about
matter:

When Mr. Whiskers beat the drum, the kids started putting things away. Soon all the kits were on the carts, and the children were sitting on the floor in front of Mr. Whiskers.

He waved his silence wand and then announced, "Raise your hand if you want to tell the class what you learned about matter."

All the kids raised their hands, and Mr. Whiskers wrote down all the things that they had to say about matter.

"So, what you're telling me," Mr. Whiskers said, "is that matter is everywhere and everything is matter. You are matter. I am matter. Everything from Popsicles to planets is matter!

"I bet you can discover all sorts of wild things about the matter in your house and out in your neighborhood too. Just don't forget to tell the rest of us about them, okay?"

The science fun was over for the day, but all the kids knew that Mr. Whiskers would bring in more strange and wonderful things to explore.

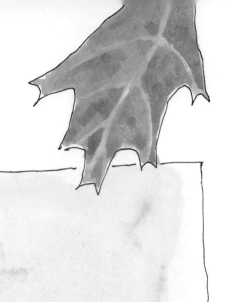

MR. WHISKERS' KIT AND CABOODLE

Do you want to do some exploring at home or in school? Here are some recipes to help you! Each tells you what materials you'll need and even sometimes where you can get them. You can store all the materials in plastic washtubs.

Have a wild time,

Mr. Whiskers

P.S. A note to adults: Kids will use the kit materials in many ways. As you listen to them and watch them, you'll learn about their discoveries.

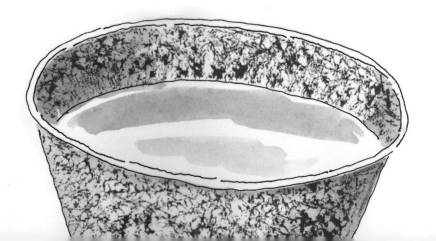

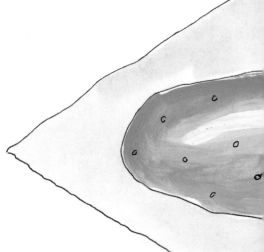

WATER DROPPERS, pages 12–15

Use plastic droppers from old medicine bottles (make sure they are washed well) or buy some droppers. (See page 45 for ordering information.) Collect some toys, and stuff like twigs, stones, or leaves to drip water on. Use food coloring to make colored water.

GLOOP, pages 16–19

It's best to play with gloop on a sheet of plastic or on an old tablecloth. Put it away in a closed container when you are done or it will dry and get hard.

1. In a large bowl, add 1 cup of water to 2 cups of white glue.
2. Fill three cups each with 1/3 cup of warm water.
3. Stir a teaspoon of borax into each cup of warm water.
4. Mix one of the cups of borax water into the glue mixture, and then add the others, one at a time. The mix will get very gloopy, but stir until all the water is mixed in.
5. Store in a plastic container with a lid.

Provide small toys, marbles, string, cups, and cookie cutters for use with the gloop.

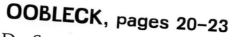

OOBLECK, pages 20–23

(Remember Dr. Seuss's *Bartholomew and the Oobleck?*)
Play with this at a picnic table outside or inside on a washable tablecloth. Have a bucket of water handy to rinse off your hands when you finish playing.

Mix 7 tablespoons of cornstarch with 4 tablespoons of water a little at a time until you get a mixture that is solid when still but melts into a liquid when held. Stir in a little green paint or food coloring. Store it in a plastic container with a lid.

ICE AND WATER, pages 24–27

This is fun to play outside on the sidewalk, blacktop, or on the patio floor.

Make some blocks of ice by freezing water in large plastic containers or gallon milk cartons. You can use old window-washer spray bottles or buy new ones at the store. Watercolor brushes or old paintbrushes work well for painting with water.

ROCKS, pages 28–31

Get pumice from your local volcano (or see page 45 for ordering information) and collect rocks from your neighborhood. Then use the things in this list to explore with: balance scale, magnifying lenses, unglazed tile, tub of water, paintbrushes.

WATER TUBS, pages 32–35

You can play with water outside in the yard or in the bathtub, where it won't matter if you get wet.

Fill a large bucket or tub with water and then use the stuff in this list to play with: funnels, corks, pebbles, pieces of pumice, balls, brushes, plastic bottles and containers, turkey basters, small toys, and sponges. At the hardware store get some two- to three-foot long pieces of acrylic tubing and some PVC pipe fittings and pipe. (They can cut the pipe into two-foot pieces for you there.)

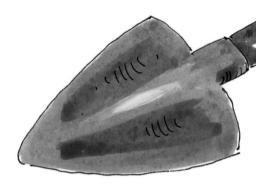

SAND AND MUD PLAY, pages 36–39

Set these materials up in a sandbox or other good digging spot: food containers of various sizes, cookie cutters and molds, large horseshoe magnet, kitchen strainers, trowels or small sand shovels, spoons or forks.

Where to order kit materials:

NASCO: Balance scales, water droppers (pipettes), magnets. 1-800-558-9595, www.homeschool-nasco.com

Carolina Biological Supply Co. 1-800-334-5551, www.carolina.com

Discount School Supply 1-800-334-2014, www.kaplanco.com

Introduction

The capital of the Republic of Hungary (Hungary to the West, but Magyarország - Land of the Magyars - to the Hungarians), Budapest is one of the most fascinating and interesting cities in Eastern Europe. Different from Moscow, different from St. Petersburg, it is paradoxically even different from itself, with its melting pot of civilizations and eras fused together with such unparalleled skill that they are sometimes indistinguishable, sometimes surprisingly evident, but always harmonious, even within the same neighborhood, the same building or the same monument.

Budapest can be envisioned as a piece of theater, an artistic work created by numerous factors that have combined to give it its substance.

The setting itself is drenched in diversity: on one side is the mountainous, hilly territory of Buda, at the same time harsh and gentle, while on the other is the enchanting plain of Pest, separated, or joined, depending on your point of view, by the waters of the great Danube. The director, the "deus ex machina," is surely history, made up of the thousand tormented episodes in which this city has played a central role. Finally, there are the actors, the true artists: its inhabitants, who proudly label themselves not Hungarians, but Magyars, and whom it would be redundant to call indomitable.

Budapest is not just an ancient city and not just a modern city. It is not a "historic" city like Rome, nor a "new" city created out of nothing, as St. Petersburg is in some respects. Rather, it is a city where destiny seems to have made numerous attempts to deny the past. Yet its inhabitants have always been able to rediscover this past, recover and return to life in a forceful and original manner. The invasions, foreign occupations, devastation and bombardments this city has suffered have proved unable to cancel out its past, and its inhabitants have always had the will and the strength to reclaim themselves, to remember, to reconstruct without ever indulging in passive nostalgia for the past, but instead amalgamating the things of yesterday with those of today, letting the ancient flow into the modern, respecting tradition and at the same time giving it new vitality. And succeeding in creating that magnificent piece of theater that is Budapest.

"Budapest is nothing but a mistake. History, which has always been a series of catastrophes here, has been a mistake. So has God, who seems to have mistaken this city for Sodom and Gomorra. And so has destiny, which has given this part of the world a language that no one understands outside its own borders [...]" This statement by the director Vajda may seem negative, yet it hides the true grandeur of Budapest, its amazing capacity to resist the vicissitudes of history, even the most negative ones, by taking the best parts and passing them on through its way of life, through the stones of its monuments, the poignant beauty of its music and the vitality of its art. Suffice it to walk along the streets near the Royal Palace in Buda to see it, to savor the ancient charm that emanates from the buildings from which medieval architectural elements peep out alongside more recent structures, from the bold approach of the very modern and hotly debated Hilton Hotel to the Matthias church, or the almost fairy tale beauty of the Fishermen's Bastion overlooking the panorama of Pest, dominated by the majestic and solemn hulk of the neo-Gothic Parliament building. Or the Oriental-style structure of the Király thermal baths and the totally 19th century luxury of the Gellért Baths, or the stupefying architecture of Ödön Lechner, not inappropriately nicknamed the Magyar Gaudí, set into the framework of the magnificent 19th century buildings that flank the roads of Pest, where neoclassical, baroque and rococo architecture triumphs. Different, yes, but in a perfectly harmonious way.

The history of Budapest has ancient roots. In fact, as early as Paleolithic times the riverbanks now occupied by Buda had human settlements which continued to develop until the Neolithic. By 2000 B.C., the opposite shore of the Danube had also been settled. More concrete historical evidence, however, begins only in the fourth century B.C., when various Celtic tribes settled the area formerly populated by Scythian peoples from southern Russia. Aravitians, Quads, Sarmatians and Marcomanns founded small villages on the banks of the river, which they called Duna, or "the great river," and began to use its bountiful waters. The presence of so many underground springs gave the territory its name - Ak-ink, or "abundant waters."

The Roman conquest of Pannonia by Druse and Tiberius signaled the end of Celtic culture for local tribes and Ak-ink and the beginning of Romanization, as witnessed by the new latinized name of the area, Aquincum. Near the original castrum, a new civilian settlement developed quite rapidly, which the Romans gave an aqueduct, paved roads, public and private buildings, thermal baths, amphitheaters and temples. In 106 A.D. the city was at the height of its development; the emperor Trajan named it capital of Lower Pannonia, Hadrian named it a municipium, and under Septimius Severus Aquincum became a colony.

Aquincum declined as rapidly as it had flourished, dragged down into the ruins of the fall of the Roman Empire, which opened the doors to incursions by barbarians from beyond the Danube. Starting in the 5th century, the area was overwhelmed by the fury of the Huns, and then the Avars. In 896 (the date Hungarians consider their nation's year of birth) the Finno-Ugric tribe of the Magyars, led by prince Árpád, crossed the Carpathians and reached the territory of Budapest, where they settled near the present site of Óbuda.

The founder of the Árpád dynasty was succeeded by great monarchs in the history of Hungary, especially prince Vajk, who was crowned in the year 1000 under the name of Stephen, and who founded a sort of feudal state. Christianity, to which he had converted as a child and which later canonized him, played an enormously important role under Stephen's rule and was imposed as a state religion, due primarily to the formidable preaching of Gellért Sagredo, the monk of Venetian origin who according to tradition was martyred on the hill of Budapest, which still bears his name (Mount Gellért). The capital of the new country was originally in Esztergom, and then moved to Székesfehérvár, but Óbuda, and with it the territory of modern Budapest, began to grow in importance.

The 13th century king Andrew II further strengthened the state feudal organization by promulgating a Golden Bull which divided the land among the nobles and established their privileges. King Béla IV transferred the capital to Buda, where the City had been built in the meantime. The last sovereign of the Árpád dynasty was Andrew III. His foreign successor, Charles of Anjou, who was backed by the pope, was crowned in Buda in 1309. Along with Louis I the Great and Sigismund of Luxembourg, who reigned until 1437, Buda entered its period of greatest flowering, marked in particular by the construction of the magnificent Royal Palace on the hill of the City. The future German emperor was succeeded first by Albert of Austria and then the "prince" of princes, Matthias Corvinus, who held the throne until 1490. The son of the famous commander János Hunyady, who routed the Turks in 1456, King Matthias was a forceful patron of the arts in Buda and founded what would become the famous Bibliotheca Corvina in the Royal Palace, which was further expanded during his reign.

The death of Matthias Corvinus signaled the beginning of Budapest's darkest hours, as it was squeezed between the worrisome presence of the Turks on its borders and the peasants' revolt, led by György Dózsa, against noble privileges. When the revolt failed, Dózsa was burned at the stake for his audacity. In 1541 the Turks, having defeated the Hungarians at Mohács, took possession of Buda and occupied the City. This was the beginning of a period of domination that continued for over one hundred and fifty years, and with the advent of Sultan Suleiman I saw the Turks installed in both Buda and Pest. The period of Turkish occupation had two clear effects on the city: on one hand destruction and cultural supremacy, which can particularly be seen in the reconversion of all churches (except for one!) into mosques, and on the other architectural transformation, exemplified by the construction of numerous Moorish-style thermal baths.

In 1686, after two years of war, the Habsburgs put an end to the Turkish domination of Óbuda, Buda and Pest, and Hungary passed under the power of the Austrian crown. This power was never suffered gladly by the inhabitants of the future capital, despite its positive aspects (including the establishment of various industries, the strengthening of trade, the opening of theaters and other cultural institutions, and the construction of new roads and important buildings).

The first signs of revolt against the Habsburgs could be seen in 1703, when prince Francis (Ferenc) Rákóczi led a popular insurrection that Vienna easily suppressed. Discontent continued to snake through the entire 18th century and exploded in the mid-19th century with the bourgeois revolution of 1848-49, in which Lajos Kossuth (the head of the revolutio-

Evocative view of the Bridge of Chains (Lánchid)

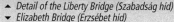

▲ *Detail of the Liberty Bridge (Szabadság híd)*
▼ *Elizabeth Bridge (Erzsébet híd)*

nary government) and the young poet Sándor Petöfi, who fell in battle, played major roles. These movements were also repressed by the central political power, which proved to be deaf to the demands of the Hungarian people for greater independence. Nevertheless, these demands became ever more pressing, until they were realized through the work of Ferenc Deák, the Magyar statesman through whose efforts the Hungarian constitution was restored and the dual monarchy of Austria-Hungary was established in 1867, with the crowning of Franz Josef I and the Empress Elizabeth. Six years later, in 1873, the administrative unification of Óbuda, Buda and Pest created the new city of Budapest.

The great economic and urban development of the capital (the Parliament building was completed in 1902) was initially shaken by social protest movements (which were forcibly suppressed) and then interrupted by the outbreak of the First World War. In 1918, at the end of the conflict, the Austro-Hungarian empire faded away, and in November it was solemnly proclaimed a republic, and was forced to cede about two thirds of its territory. The next year a coalition of social democrats and Communists (Republic of Councils) led by Béla Kun took power, but only six months later it was replaced by the government of admiral Miklós Horty, who began restoration in a climate of terror. On the waves of a resurgence in nationalistic spirit, in 1938 Hungary signed the Nazi racial laws and in 1941, after attacking Yugoslavia, allied itself with Hitler's Germany, on whose side it fought during the Second World War. The war brought death and destruction to Budapest, devastating more than 70 percent of its buildings and in many cases razing buildings and monuments to the ground. Liberation from the Nazis cost the soldiers of the Soviet Red Army dearly - they paid for the victory of February 13, 1945 with 80,000 lives.

With the Yalta peace agreement Hungary passed under the power of Moscow, and in 1949 the republic became a people's republic led by Mátyás Rákosi, with a Stalinist-style constitution. The revolution of 1956 seemed to put an end to the dark years of this period, as the Imre Nagy government was installed, Hungary was proclaimed a neutral government and it withdrew from the Warsaw Pact. But the Soviet reaction was immediate and violent: its tanks entered Budapest, Nagy (who was executed in 1958) was replaced by János Kadár, and hopes for freedom seemed permanently quashed. But in 1989 the Hungarian "velvet revolution" began, which led to the destruction of the Iron Curtain at the border of Austria and the proclamation of the new Hungarian Republic based on democracy.

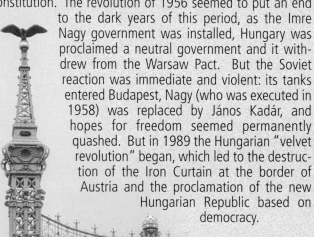

◄ *View of the Liberty Bridge (Szabadság híd)*

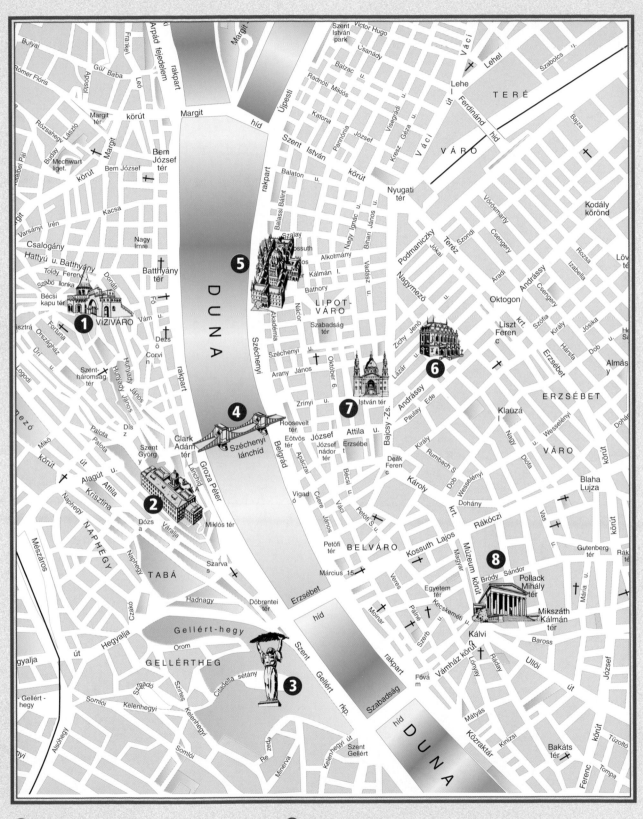

1. Fishermen's Bastion
2. The Royal Palace
3. Monument to the Liberation
4. The Bridge of Chains
5. The Parliament
6. Opera House
7. Basilica of St. Stephen
8. National Museum

Obuda

Located in the far north of Budapest on the right bank of the Danube, Óbuda (or Old Buda) was the oldest of the three autonomous cities (which included Óbuda, Buda and Pest) that were united in 1873, creating the present-day capital. The oldest remains found in its territory in fact date back to prehistoric times, while the vestiges of the settlement the Romans founded on the site date back to a few years after the birth of Christ.

The present-day center of Óbuda was once a military castrum, near which a true city, Aquincum (from the Celtic Ak-Ink, or abundant waters), soon developed, with various buildings, paved roads, city walls and a three story aqueduct.

The settlement, which the emperor Trajan named the capital of eastern Pannonia, became a municipality in 124 A.D. under Hadrian, and in 194 A.D. a colony under Septimius Severus. Destroyed in the second century by barbarians, the flourishing city was assaulted by the Huns numerous times during the 4th century, and slowly lost its importance and was abandoned. Archeological excavations begun in the late 19th century revealed numerous remains of the ancient city which are now on display in the Archeological Museum located on the site. Some of the buildings of Aquincum have also been discovered, including the foundations of the private homes and the streets, the public baths, the Basilica, the temple of Mithras, the Macellum, the remains of the aqueduct and two amphitheaters, an enormous one in the military city (its arena is larger than that of the Coliseum) and the other in the civilian city. A luxurious private villa has also been discovered nearby.

Dating from the 3rd century A.D., it is decorated with splendid mosaics from the cycle of Hercules, which have given the building its name.

With the decay of the Roman city, Óbuda was occupied by the Huns, whose king Attila seems to have made his residence

Details of the Aquincum

there. The fortunes of the city, which improved significantly under the Árpád dynasty and in the Middle Ages as well, were interrupted during the domination of the Turks, who had shifted their interest to the nearby Buda. Some of the most famous vestiges of this period include the Király Baths along Fő utca, built by the Turks around 1570. One can admire the oldest portion of the elegant building, with the original octagonal tub covered with a cupola and other spa areas covered with three smaller cupolas. In the nineteenth century the baths passed into the hands of the royal family, giving them the name of Király, which means King in Hungarian. The baths were enlarged and restored after the Second World War.

In the 17th century Óbuda began to thrive again, but it was able to retain its own character without being assimilated into the glories of Buda. While this character is perhaps more modest, it is certainly no less rich in charm, with

Király Baths on Fő utca

its elegant period residences, neat little tenement houses, small inns and romantic streets.

The reconstruction of the city completed in the late 1960's radically changed its appearance but fortunately did not completely destroy it, preserving the beautiful Fő tér square.

The square, decorated with a curious group of bronze statues by Imre Varga entitled Women in the Rain (1923), is overlooked by the elegant Zichy Castle. Built in baroque style between 1746 and 1757 by the Zichy family (which also built the Óbuda parish church during the same period), the palace, restored after the Second World War, now holds a cultural center which includes the Óbuda History Museum, the Lajos Kassák Museum (a famous member of the Hungarian avant-garde in the early 20th century) and the Victor Vasarely Museum (named after a famous contemporary painter), as well as temporary shows and concerts.

The City Hall and numerous characteristic bars and restaurants are also located on Fő tér square, including the Postakocsi Restaurant.

Details of Aquincum

B ut beyond the "retro" charm of Fő tér square, Óbuda provides visitors with other interesting testimony of its history, including the remains of the Roman baths in Flórián tér, another large square in the city, or, nearby, the remains of the queen's castle built in medieval times. There is also the synagogue (today a cultural center), built in neoclassical style in 1820, and the so-called Oval House, a spinning mill built in the late 19th century when the village was being industrialized. The Kiscelli Museum, located on the hill of the same name, also offers a broad panorama of the history of the three cities (Óbuda, Buda and Pest), which in the late 19th century combined to form the present-day capital. The museum, which includes a portion of the Historical Museum, contains an important collection of period objects and documents displayed in the halls of an old convent. The building, decorated by a splendid baroque gate, was built in the 18th century for the Trinitarian monks, and also serves as a funeral chapel for the Zichy family, rich landowners of Óbuda.

Óbuda, Fő tér: statue of Imre Varga ▶

Entry to the Postakocsi Restaurant in the Fő Building , Óbuda ▼

Buda

Built on the plateau lying on the right bank of the Danube, the city, dominated by the hill of the Royal Palace, is the most fascinating part of the Magyar capital, the best place to witness its complex historical vicissitudes and a precious display case for its artistic and architectural life.

Originally a refuge for those threatened by the barbarians, when it offered underground shelters, in the 13th century Buda became the residence of the Hungarian kings and was fortified and provided with houses and public civil and religious buildings. A protagonist of the tormented historical and political upheavals of the Middle Ages, during the Renaissance the city experienced a period of peace and great artistic and cultural flowering under the reign of Matthias Corvinus, which was followed by the dark period of Turkish domination and the advent of the Habsburgs.

The Second World War seemed to wreak all its violence on Buda, devastating almost all its monuments and leav-

▲ *Kapisztrán Square: detail*
▼ *Royal Palace - Király Palota*

ing wounds that seemed impossible to heal. But heal they did. The city was entirely rebuilt and its buildings restored with incredible care and attention, so that even the oldest buildings and details (from medieval, Gothic and Renaissance periods) that seemed to have been canceled from history were brought back to life at the end of the war. Due to this work, which is extraordinary not only from the architectural and historical perspective, but above all as a testimony of the determination of the capital's residents and their love for their city and their history, Buda is now one of the world's cultural assets protected by UNESCO.

One reaches the city of Buda from Óbuda by following Fő utca, which leads to Clark Ádám tér, overlooking the Bridge of Chains.

▲ *Royal Palace - Király Palota*

The route winds through the part of the city called Vizíváros, the "city of waters" lying between the hill and the banks of the Danube. Particularly interesting due to the presence of important baroque (including the churches of St. Ann and St. Elizabeth and the chapel of St. Florian) and rococo monuments, the district is also a witness to the period of Turkish domination, during which the pashas embellished the spa buildings (the Király Baths) and transformed numerous churches into mosques (such as the former Capuchin convent on Corvin tér).

In Clark Ádám tér, named after the English engineer who built the Bridge of Chains (Széchenyi lánchíd) between 1838 and 1849 and in 1857 built the Alagút, the tunnel which passes through the hill to reach the neighborhoods behind it, is the bizarre Monument at km 0, a modern milestone that indicates the point from which the distances of the streets to and from Budapest are measured. From here one can go up to the Royal Palace area in the beautiful cable car, or sikló, built in 1870, that leads to Szent György tér, on the southern side of the hill.

▲ *Clark ÁDAM tér*

▲ SIKLO - Clark Ádám tér: cable car

◀ Halászo Gyerekek (boys fishermen)

▼ Royal Palace southern gate

15

On the square, embellished with a fountain depicting King Matthias (1904), stands the majestic Royal Palace (Várpalota), which holds the history of Buda within its walls. During the second half of the 13th century Béla IV used this site for his residence, which was nevertheless destroyed. A century later Charles Albert of Anjou ordered the construction of a small castle on the hill, but it was not until the time of King Sigismund that a fortified royal palace was built. This Gothic-style palace was modified, expanded and enriched by King Matthias, who used great architects and artists for the work and who also built the great hall for the library, one of the most complete of its times, with over 2500 volumes. With the Turkish occupation the palace lost its splendor, and during the siege of 1686 it was destroyed. A new building constructed in the early

18th century was then expanded under the empress Maria Theresa and during the period of Count Palatine, when it assumed the shape of a large, single building formed of two symmetrical blocks connected by a central structure crowned with a cupola. During the Second World War the Royal Palace was razed to the ground. Its reconstruction, which began in 1950, returned the building to its original form and at the same time highlighted the presence of medieval and Renaissance features discovered during the course of the work. Its interior was extensively changed to provide room for the important museums now located in the Royal Palace: the National Hungarian Gallery (a true temple of Hungarian art from the Middle Ages to the present), the Budapest Historical Museum (which also contains splendid examples of Gothic statues and includes the elegant Palatine chapel adorned by a 15th century triptych), the Workers' Movement Museum and the enormous National Library.

Nighttime view of the Royal Palace

▼ *Royal Palace: statue of Jenő Savoyai*

▲ *Church of St. Matthias: detail*

Leaving the Royal Palace, from Szent György tér turn right on Színház utca, the street on which the Palace Theater is located. This building, built as a convent in the 13th century, was a residence for the pashas during the Turkish occupation, and was not transformed into a theater until the late 18th century. Destroyed in 1944-45, it was reopened in 1978. The road runs into Dísz tér, the medieval market square, decorated with monuments to heroes of the movements of 1848-49 and surrounded by beautiful baroque buildings with elements dating back to the Middle Ages. The Korona pastry shop at number 16 is the oldest in the capital.

Continuing along Tárnok utca, a medieval street embellished by 15th and 16th century architecture (note the old Golden Eagle Pharmacy at number 8, now a museum), come to the splendid Trinity Square (Szentháromság tér). The baroque monument in the center, the Trinity Column, was erected by Catholics in gratitude for having escaped the peril of the plague epidemics of the 17th and 18th centuries. On the

left side of the square is the old City Hall of Buda (1703), while the opposite side is dominated by the church of Our Lady, better known as the Matthias church (Mátyás-templom). Recognizable by its façade with the Romanesque gate and splendid bas-relief in colored granite flanked by two bell towers - the Béla bell tower (the smaller one) and the Gothic-style Matthias bell tower, bearing the king's coat of arms (1470) - the church was built in the mid-13th century. During the 14th and the 15th centuries it was expanded, with the addition of the choirs and the side chapels and the Matthias tower (80 m tall). Transformed into a mosque during the Turkish occupation, it then passed to the Jesuits and took on its present appearance through restoration work begun in 1874. The extremely rich interior with a nave and two aisles is decorated with frescoes, stained glass, sculptures and elegant geometric paintings.

◀ *Column of the Holy Trinity*

▶ *Church of St. Matthias*
▶ *Church of St. Matthias: interior*

L eaving the church, on the southern end of the square one can admire the equestrian statue of St. Stephen (1906), the first king of Hungary and the founder of the Magyar state. Behind the monument is the white marble hulk of the Fishermen's Bastion (Halászbástya).

This bizarre neo-Romanesque complex was built between 1899 and 1903 by the architect Frigyes Schulek on the hill which in medieval times was occupied by a guild of fishermen, who also held their fish market here. The Bastion, which has been criticized by many as a dissonant element in the otherwise harmonious architectural panorama of the hill district, offers a spectacular view of the city and the banks of the Danube.

Another hotly debated and criticized work in the Royal Palace area is the Hilton Hotel, located behind the Matthias church and the site of the Budapest Casino.

The building, constructed on Hess András tér in 1976 and based on a design by Béla Pintér, has the peculiarity

▲ *Fisherman Bastion: detail*

of an extremely modern structure that nevertheless encompasses elements of a medieval Dominican convent and church which were revealed during the construction of the hotel. Thus, the old Nicholas Tower has found a new and singular location among the mirrored walls of the complex, alongside a reproduction of a Gothic bas-relief depicting the effigy of Matthias Corvinus.

Equestrian Statue of St. Stephen

View of the Bastion ▶
Fisherman Bastion: detail ▶

The square named after Hess András (the typographer who printed the first book in Hungary in 1473) is embellished by a statue of Pope Innocent XI, who in 1686 played a decisive role in liberating Buda, and includes interesting neoclassical buildings standing alongside medieval houses which retain splendid Gothic-style elements. Note in particular the former Red Porcupine Inn (where the first theatrical works in Buda were presented in the 18th century) and the building which houses the Fortuna Restaurant. Examples of similar architecture in baroque, rococo and classical style, now classified as monuments, can also be found along Táncsics Mihály utca (in medieval times the Jewish quarter) and on the parallel streets Fortuna utca and Országház utca. Following the first of these streets one reaches Bécsi kapu tér, where one can still admire the Vienna gate, the only one of the original gates of the city which escaped demolition. On the square, which in medieval times was the site of the Saturday market, are several interesting buildings, including the majestic neo-Romanesque National Archives.

▲ ▼ *Fortuna Street (Fortuna utca)*

National Archives Building

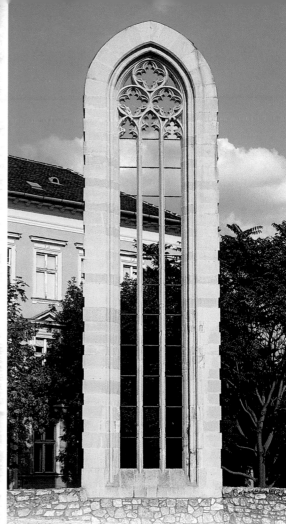

▲ Remains of the church of St. Mary Magdalene in Kapisztrán Square

◄ Remains of the Dominican church next to the Hilton Hotel; statue of King Matthias

▼ Kapisztrán Square: bell tower of the church of St. Mary Magdalene

From here, turning left on Petermann Biró utca, one comes to Kapisztrán tér, named after Juan de Capistrano, the monk who was a friend of János Hunyady, who defeated the Turks in 1456 and was the father of Matthias Corvinus. Near the monument to Capistrano in the great square is the Military History Museum, located within a vast neoclassical building formerly utilized as a barracks. Behind the complex one can admire the Bastion of the Anjous and follow the communications trench of the Tóth Árpád sétány walls, which offers a fabulous view of the hills of Buda. The Gothic bell tower of the church of St. Mary Magdalene, built in 1276, is also located on Kapisztrán tér. The bombardments of the Second World War left nothing but the foundations of this church, the only one which remained open during the Turkish occupation.

To return to the Royal Palace, follow narrow Úri utca (Lords' Street), dotted with baroque buildings with splendid Romanesque and Gothic architectural elements from the medieval houses on which foundations they were built.

Military Museum

Marxin Restaurant

▼ *Houses on Úri Str.*

Souvenir shop at the Castle ▲

▼ *Fortress Street: details*

▲ Gellért Baths

◄ Monument to the Soviet in Szabadság

Leaving the Royal Palace hill, one can reach the Elizabeth Bridge (1961-64) and climb up Mount Gellért. The mountain, in reality a dolomitic hill 235 meters high, is one of the most enchanting parkland areas of the city (the side facing the Danube offers spectacular views of Budapest, while the opposite side, where vineyards once grew, is the site of the lovely Jubilee Park), but also contains important monuments. The name of the mountain comes from bishop Gellért, who during the time of Stephen I began the Christianization of the Magyars.

A monument dedicated to the saint was built where, according to tradition, he was martyred in 1046. From here, a walkway leads to the top of the mountain, which is occupied by the Citadel, the fortress built by the Austrians in 1851, and where a century later the Germans battled Soviet soldiers. To commemorate the sacrifice of the latter and the victory of the Red Army, the great monument to the Liberation was built in 1947.

The slopes of Mount Gellért are full of healing hot springs. They have been used since the Middle Ages and supply some of the most famous thermal baths in the city: the Gellért baths, famous for their elegant early 20th century architecture and the luxurious decoration of their rooms, which are equipped with the most modern spa facilities; the Rudas baths, located in an Oriental-

style building (the Turks expanded it in the 16th century) distinguished by its cupola with stained glass windows; and the Rác baths, which also show Ottoman influence. The first two complexes are near the Liberty Bridge and the Elizabeth Bridge respectively, while the Rác baths are in the old Tabán quarter, located between the mountain and the Royal Palace hill and now covered by broad parklands.

▾ *Rác Baths*

Monument to the Liberation ▸

Tular Madár

Pest

On the opposite bank of the Danube, Pest, which has long lived in the shadow of the nearby royal city (to which it was annexed only in 1873), underwent its greatest period of growth in the 19th century, as the luxurious and in some cases daring architecture of many of its buildings attests. At that time it began to grow increasingly important in economic, political and administrative life. Nevertheless, it should not be forgotten that the city was quite important even in Roman times (the Romans founded the castrum of Contra Aquincum for the precise purpose of controlling river traffic), and that even later it continued to play an important role in the history of the future capital, with its greatest period of enrichment and expansion during the Renaissance and 18th century.

The boundary marked by the fortified walls and the defensive moat of the old city, now the historic center contained within Kiskörút (Little Avenue), a network of roads that starts from the Liberty Bridge and runs in a semicircle until returning to the Danube on Deák Ferenc utca, dates back to the 15th century. In the heart of the old center of Pest and located parallel to the river, Váci utca is certainly the most lively and elegant street in Budapest, along which the most exclusive shops, department stores and cafés in the city are located.

Palace detail on Szabadság square
Pizza Jazz Restaurant on Váci Street

Statue of Hermes before the Fontana Shopping Centre in Régiposta Street

CAFÉ & RESTAURANT NEW YORK
1894
HUNGARY BUDAPEST

New York Café   *New York Café Sign*

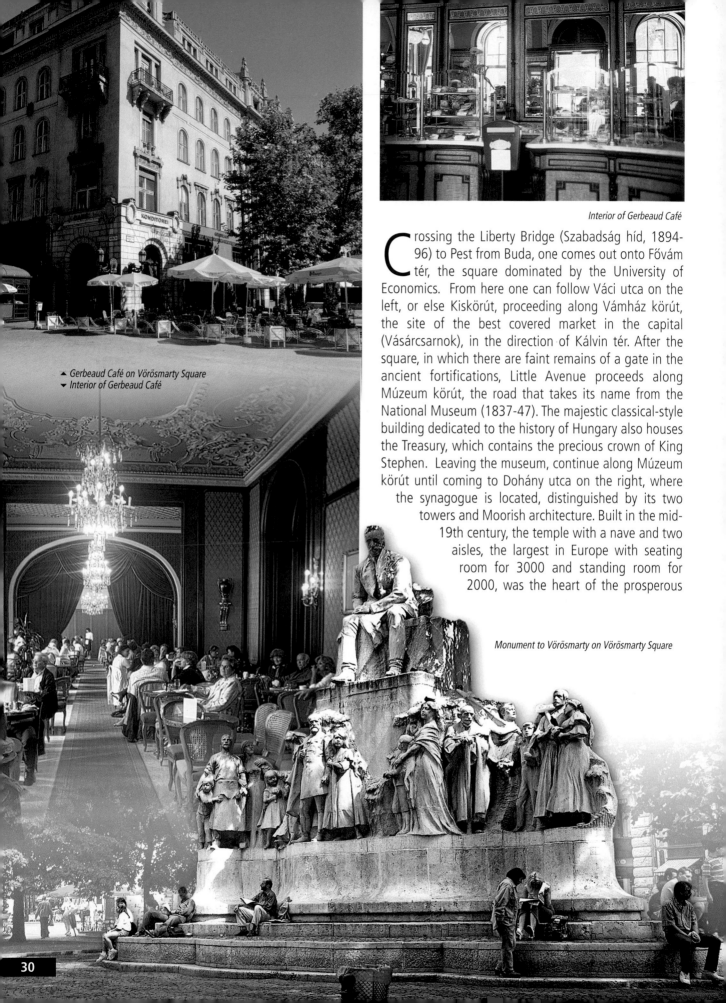

Interior of Gerbeaud Café

▲ *Gerbeaud Café on Vörösmarty Square*
▼ *Interior of Gerbeaud Café*

Crossing the Liberty Bridge (Szabadság híd, 1894-96) to Pest from Buda, one comes out onto Fővám tér, the square dominated by the University of Economics. From here one can follow Váci utca on the left, or else Kiskörút, proceeding along Vámház körút, the site of the best covered market in the capital (Vásárcsarnok), in the direction of Kálvin tér. After the square, in which there are faint remains of a gate in the ancient fortifications, Little Avenue proceeds along Múzeum körút, the road that takes its name from the National Museum (1837-47). The majestic classical-style building dedicated to the history of Hungary also houses the Treasury, which contains the precious crown of King Stephen. Leaving the museum, continue along Múzeum körút until coming to Dohány utca on the right, where the synagogue is located, distinguished by its two towers and Moorish architecture. Built in the mid-19th century, the temple with a nave and two aisles, the largest in Europe with seating room for 3000 and standing room for 2000, was the heart of the prosperous

Monument to Vörösmarty on Vörösmarty Square

and lively ghetto (Erzsébetváros), as can be seen in the buildings which dot the streets, until the Nazis came to power and its inhabitants were decimated. The Mausoleum for Jews fallen in the First World War and the Jewish Museum are annexed to the synagogue. Continuing along Kiskörút, one reaches Deák Ferenc tér, the square where the three lines of the Budapest subway system meet and a unique underground museum is located.

From here follow Deák Ferenc utca to Vörösmarty tér, the true center of Pest. The square is dominated by the marble monument to the great 19th century poet who gave it its name and is famous for the Gerbeaud pastry shop, renowned both for its specialties and its splendid interior.

▲ General markets on Fővám Square
▼ A building on the corner of Vörösmarty Tér and Déak Utce

Synagogue on Dohány Street ▶

The Vigadó

The previously mentioned Váci utca begins from the square, and at this point, before going along the backs of the Danube, it is worth the effort to follow the stretch of road that leads to the Elizabeth Bridge (Erzsébet híd, 1961-64) and go to Március 15 tér, where the remains of Contra Aquincum may be found. Facing the square is the parish church of the Center, built prior to the 11th century on the remains of the Roman castrum. It became the principal church of Pest in the 12th century, and in the 15th century was expanded and given a new Gothic shape. Like nearly all the churches of the city, it was transformed into a mosque during the Turkish domination. Restored various times (first in baroque style, then classical, then Gothic), the building was devastated during the Second World War and restored after 1948, when its Gothic and baroque styles were given predominance.

From Március 15 tér one can return toward Vörösmarty tér by crossing Petöfi tér (with its splendid Greek Orthodox church) and following the lovely walk along the Danube. At the luxurious Hotel Marriott and Forum, facing the enchanting panorama of Buda's Royal Palace hill, one of the most architecturally interesting buildings of Pest rises imposingly: the Vigadó. Built in 1859-64, the late Romantic style palace was designed to host chamber music and theater, and concerts by Liszt, Brahms, Debussy and Bartók were performed here. The exterior, destroyed by a fire during the last war, was restored to its original form, retaining the structure of the splendid façade with columns and semi-columns alternating with large arched windows inserted with friezes, allegorical figures and statues of characters from Hungarian history. The interior was restored based on a more modern design.

From Vigadó tér continue along the walk that follows the Danube to the Bridge of Chains, where the grandiose Roosevelt tér opens out. Originally the square was simply known as the market square, because an open air market was held there. In the mid-19th century, when construction of the bridge was complet-ed, it was renamed the Bridge of Chains square, and only after the Second World War did it receive its present name, in honor of the President of the United States at that time, Franklin Delano Roosevelt. The square is embellished by a garden decorated with two statues: that of István Széchenyi, the founder of the nearby

Gresham Building

Academy of the Sciences, and that of the 19th century statesman Ferenc Deák.

On the eastern side of Roosevelt tér is the majestic Gresham building, easily recognizable by its imposing façade in stone decorated with relief work. The building, in pure secessionist style, was built in 1907 based on a design by the architects Quittner and Vágó, who also designed the inner gallery. Originally the headquarters of the London insurance company of the same name, between the World War I and World War II the Gresham building housed the Gresham Café, the preferred meeting place for numerous artists in the capital.

The other large monument that faces Roosevelt tér is the Hungarian Academy of the Sciences (Magyar Tudományos Akadémia), an imposing building in neo-Renaissance style built in 1864 based on a design by Friedrich August Stüler, a German architect. The main façade, which is rather severe, is embellished by six statues representing the various sectors in which the institution was originally divided (law, science, mathematics, philosophy, languages and history). Other allegorical depictions (archeology, poetry, astronomy and political science) decorate the side of the Academy facing the Danube, while the corners of the building depict famous scientists. The history of the birth of the Academy is closely bound to its patron, Count István Széchenyi (1792-1860), a politician and reformer who promoted the establishment of an institution entirely devoted to the study of the Hungarian language and its literature. Széchenyi, whose generosity was soon imitated by other city personalities, offered a sum of money equivalent to a year's earnings from his estates in order to create the Academy, which was thus established in 1825. Its foundation has been immortalized in the 1893 bronze bas-relief which decorates the facade. Ever since its creation, the Academy has continued to expand its fields of interest, and, due in part to its enormous scientific library, has become a renowned research center for scholars the world over.

Near the Academy of the Sciences is the pleasant Akadémia utca, an interesting street primarily due to the architecture that characterizes several of its buildings. In particular, buildings 1 and 3, built in the first half of the 19th century, are especially noteworthy for their pure classic style.

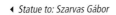

◀ Statue to: Szarvas Gábor

▶ View of the Hungarian Academy

Zrínyi utca runs from Roosevelt tér and soon reaches Szent István tér, the square where the majestic Basilica, the name which the inhabitants give to the church of St. Stephen, is located. The grandiose building was begun in 1848, but work was immediately interrupted by the outbreak of the war of independence. In 1851 the famous architect József Hild recommenced work on the building, which is distinguished by a particularly tormented history.

Hild gave the building a decidedly classical look and nearly finished it before he died in 1868. Nevertheless, that same year the cupola of the building collapsed and reconstruction work was assigned to another famous architect of the time, Miklós Ybl, who reshaped the Basilica into a neo-Renaissance style. After Ybl's death, the building was completed in 1905 by József Kauser, who gave it its baroque interior by changing the designs of the architects

◄ Sas utca

who had preceded him.

Crowned by the great, 96 meter high central cupola and flanked by two 80 meter high bell towers, the church, with its Greek cross design, is exceptionally large, 86 meters long by 55 meters wide. Worthy of note on the outside are the statues which decorate the edifice, in particular those of the Twelve Apostles on the outside wall of the apse above the semicircular colonnade, the work of Leó Fessler, and the figures of the Four Evangelists located in the outside niches at the base of the cupola.

The solemn interior is richly adorned by statues (those at the base of the pillars on which the cupola rests are of particular note), paintings (including the famous work by Gyula Benczúr which depicts St. Stephen offering the Virgin Mary the crown of Hungary) and the bronze relief work that crowns the splendid Venetian mosaics of the cupola.

▼ Basilica of St. Stephen

Auditorium ▲

Foyer with double marble staircase ▼

Opera House

From the basilica of St. Stephen continue a short way on the nearby Andrássyut, the straight street that leads to Hősök tere and leads to the State Opera House (Állami Operaház), a majestic building in neo-Renaissance style built between 1875 and 1884 based on a design by Miklós Ybl.

On the first floor of the principal façade is an elegant loggia with niches on both sides decorated by allegorical statues of the muses of dance, love poetry, comedy and tragedy, while on the second floor terrace the balustrade contains statues of famous musicians and composers.

The main entrance, flanked by statues of Franz Liszt and Ferenc Erkel (the Opera's first director and the author of the Hungarian national anthem), leads into the sumptuous foyer with a double marble staircase with walls and ceiling decorated by precious frescoes and paintings. The marvelous auditorium, one of the most elegant in Europe, has perfect acoustics and covers three levels, with the royal box on the first level (the salon now contains a museum of the history of the Opera).

The ceiling is decorated with elegant frescoes by Károly Lotz depicting Apollo, the god of music, at the center of Olympus, while the walls contain beautiful murals by Mór Than.

View of the Opera House

Parliament

From Szent István tér, proceeding north on Sas utca or one of the parallel roads leading toward the Parliament area, one reaches the vast Szabadság tér, or Liberty Square, the great green lungs of the quarter. This square was built in the early 20th century on an area which until 1898 contained a barracks sadly famous for having been the site of the executions of numerous Hungarian heroes during the 1848 war of independence.

The grandiose square is crowned by the splendid buildings that line it, all quite large and architecturally interesting.

One example is the yellowish Hungarian Television building (page 57), formerly the Stock Exchange, constructed in secessionist style with art nouveau decorations, and the National Bank of Hungary building, designed, as was the former, by the architect Ignác Alpár, but this time in late eclectic style. Next to the National Bank of Hungary is the highly original building of the former Postal Savings Bank, built in 1900 by the great architect Ödön Lechner, who, as in other surprising works, was able to elegantly combine materials such as colored majolica and brick. In the center of the gardens of the square is an obelisk (1945) commemorating the Soviet soldiers who died during the liberation of Budapest.

Views of the Parliament

Leaving Liberty Square, proceed down short Vécsey utca, and passing the statue of Imre Nagy (page 47), come to Kossuth Lajos tér, another large square, famous primarily because it is the site of the monumental Parliament building (Országház). The square is named after the Hungarian politician who was one of the leading figures of the 1848 uprisings. A commemorative monument to him dating from 1952 stands on the square, opposite a 1935 equestrian statue on the other side depicting another great hero of national independence, the Hungarian prince Ferenc Rákóczi II. A beautiful statue created in 1980 by the sculptor László Marton is dedicated to the poet József Attila and is located on the southern side of the Parliament building.

With its grandiose proportions (268 meters long by 118 meters wide), the spectacular building (known to the inhabitants of Budapest as the People's House) was built between the end of the 19th century and the beginning of the 20th century (1884-1906) based on a design by Imre Steindl, with the precise intent of becoming one of the city's main

Views of the Parliament

A Statue of Im Nagy ▼

symbols. With its statues (more than 200 of them), its spires and its little loggias, the great windows and arches in pure neo-Gothic style, its gigantic cupola (96 meters high like that of the nearby basilica of St. Stephen) and its breathtaking architecture overlooking the waters of the Danube, the building is one of the most fascinating focal points of the city. It consists of a central structure, covered by the cupola and embellished by the splendid loggia on the main fa-çade, surrounded by high towers, and two side structures with corners decorated by small towers that contain the congress hall on the north and the deputy meeting room on the south, both of which are sump-tuously decorated.

Visits to Parliament, possible only if accompanied by a guide, are limited to particular times, depending on the duties of the organs of government which operate in the building. Within the palace, which includes fully ten courtyards, there are 691 halls, many of which are decorated by paintings (those of the Hungarian kings in the luxurious cupola-shaped hall on the first floor are interesting, as well as the splendid Conquest by Mihály Munkácsy in the room named after him), frescoes, tapestries (an entire hall is decorated

View of the Parliament

Statue of Attila József

RECRVDESCVNT DIVTINA
INCLYTÆ GENTIS HVNGARÆ
VULNERA

by rare Gobelin tapestries) and statues, and are richly embellished by refined furnishings.

In addition to the monumental Parliament building, Kossuth Lajos tér is surrounded by other important buildings, primary among which is that which houses the Ethnographic Museum. This majestic neoclassical structure, built in 1896, was in the past the site of the court building, as shown by the chariot drawn by horses with the goddess of Justice depicted above the timpanum of the elegant main façade interspersed with six columns.

The entrance to the halls, where objects from both Hungary and other countries are on display, is preceded by a splendid staircase adorned by marble and frescoes. Continue north from the Parliament building and follow the Danube riverside walk to Jászai Mari tér, where the Margaret Bridge begins.

From the bridge, which was built immediately after the Bridge of Chains in
1872-76, was destroyed by the Nazis
during the war and was rebuilt in 1949, one
enters Szent István körút. This avenue is part
of the Great Ring Road (Nagykörút), opened
in 1896 during the Millennium celebrations,
which winds in semicircular fashion for four
kilometers along Szent István
körút, Teréz and Erzsébet
körút, József and
Ferenc körút, cross-
ing Pest from the
Margaret Bridge to
the Petőfi

▲ *Nyugati Station* ▶

▼ *Buda: the little "Pioneers"
train*

Bridge to the south. At Szent István körút number 14 is the Vígszínház, the Prose Theater, built in 1896.

The building was almost entirely destroyed during by fire during World War II, but it was soon rebuilt, and its outer facade was restored to its original neo-baroque style. The interior was radically changed, however, using more modern criteria. Proceeding along the avenue, come to Marx tér, dominated by the modern glass building of the Skála Metro shops and the splendid Nyugati Pályaudvar, the West Train Station. The elegant building, listed as one of Hungary's cultural assets, was built in 1874-77 by the Parisian company Eiffel based on a design by architects August De Serres and Gyozo Bernard, who are responsible for the refined combination of iron and glass that predominates on the main façade.

Hősök Tere/Városliget

Continuing along the Great Ring Road, come octogon where Nagy körút intersects Andrássy str., which leads to Hősök tere. The first part of the avenue designed by architects Ybl and Linzenbauer in 1872, between Bajcsy-Zsilinszky út and Kodály körönd, is flanked by elegant buildings and sumptuous palaces, while the last portion, between Kodály körönd and Hősök tere, is dotted with splendid villas immersed in green lawns and runs into the Városliget municipal park. The construction of the vast Hősök tere, or Heroes' Square, began in 1896, the year in which the Millennium Show celebrated the one thousand year anniversary of the Magyar conquest of the country. The work, concluded in 1929, was entrusted to Fülöp Herzog and Albert Schickedanz, the architect who, along with the sculptor György Zala, also designed the grandiose monument to the Millennium that crowns the square. Flanked by two semicircular colonnades decorated by statues, a column 36 meters high overlooks the statue of the archangel Gabriel, while at its base are groups of sculptures depicting Prince Árpád and six commanders who led the conquest of the country.

Views and details of Heroes' Square (Hősök tere)

Details of the Mücsarnok Museum on Hősök Square

According to the design of Schickedanz and Herzog, the square was to include two imposing, majestic buildings which would provide the crowning touch. Of the two, both by Schickedanz, the first to be constructed was the Art Gallery (Műcsarnok). The building is a combination of two popular architectural styles of the time, classicist, as evidenced in its beautiful, regular lines, and eclectic, evident in the combination of red brick and colored majolica decorations. In addition to the biennial, the Gallery contains temporary art shows. On the other side is the monumental Museum of Fine Arts (Szépművészeti Múzeum), built in 1906 in neo-classical style with a portico of Corinthian columns decorated with a timpanum

▲ Museum of Fine Arts (Szépművészeti múzeum)
◀ Details of the Műcsarnok Museum on Hősök Square

with a bas-relief inspired by that of the temple of Zeus in Olympia. The museum, the largest in Hungary and one of the major museums of the world, contains precious collections (from Greek and Roman art to Hungarian and foreign art of the 20th century) that include an extensive representation of Italian Renaissance works.

Behind Heroes' Square is a large park, the most beautiful and perhaps the most popu-lar in Budapest, Városliget. An extension of Andrássy ut runs down the center of this park, which also includes a lake and which features various attractions (recreation areas, refreshment areas, museums, thermal baths, a splendid zoo and an amusement park) that throughout the year attract thousands of visitors and inhabitants of the capital looking for a bit of relaxation and fun. Built between the late 18th century and the 19th century on what was originally swampland, Városliget was de-signed by the French landscape architect Henrik Nebbien in the late 19th century. Located in the center of the lake on little Széchenyi Island, the main attraction of the park is Vajdahunyad Castle, which combines all the principal architectural styles in Hungary within its various build-ings.

▲ *Vajdahunyad Castle in Városliget Park*

Statue of the Archer ▶

◀ *Anonymous monument in Városliget Park*

Originally the castle was built in papier-mâché for the Millennium celebrations, and only later was it transformed into a permanent structure by the architect Ignác Álpár (commemorated by a statue at the entrance to the building).

The castle which gives its name to the entire complex may be traced to that owned by János Hunyady in Transylvania. The two towers at the sides of the entrance are reproductions of old towers of Hungary and Romania. On the outside, the jak chapel is an imitation of a Benedictine church in a village in the western part of the country, and other buildings use Hungarian and Transylvanian construction styles. Finally, a baroque-style building houses the interesting Museum of Agriculture, before which stands the monument to Anonymous. Unveiled in 1903, it is dedicated to the anonymous 13th century chronicler, whom some have identified as a counselor of King Béla III, who compiled the Gesta Hungarorum.

Immediately behind the Museum of Fine Arts, north of Vajdahunyad Castle, is the famous Gundel Restaurant, located in an elegant liberty-style building adorned with an enchanting flower garden. A short distance away, a richly decorated gate resting on the statues of two elephants opens onto the splendid Zoological Gardens. Opened in 1866, the zoo contains over 500 species of animals, most of which are housed in liberty-style buildings, a beautiful iron greenhouse (the Palm House) built by the Parisian company Eiffel in the late 19th century and a pleasant botanical garden with about 1500 species of plants. Next to the Zoological Gardens are two more attractions: the permanent Budapest circus (1971) and Vidám Park, the great amusement park built in 1878. On the eastern side of Városliget one can visit the interesting Communications Garden, a bicycle path created especially for children, and the Transport Museum, dedicated to the history of transport in Hungary from ancient times to the present. It contains models of trams, locomotives, boats and airplanes.

Gundel Restaurant in Városliget ▲
The Hungarian Television Building ▼

Within Városliget Park, right in front of the Circus in the northern area, is one of the most famous thermal baths in Budapest, the Széchenyi Baths (Széchenyi fürdő). The baths are located in a sumptuous palace built in 1909 based on a design by Győző Czigler, who did not skimp on stucco work, gold and profuse decorations, in perfect rococo style, that adorn the entry and spa of the complex. The baths include an indoor swimming pool with various pools at different temperatures, sauna rooms, and an enormous outdoor swimming pool, behind which stands the splendid neo-classical building. The hot baths are fed by a natural spring of curative hot water (70°C), which had already been discovered in the 1870's by the geologist Zsigmondy. Like the other thermal baths in the capital, the outdoor pool of the Széchenyi Baths is extremely popular throughout the year.

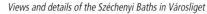

Views and details of the Széchenyi Baths in Városliget

Margaret Island

Located in the middle of the Danube at the level of Óbuda between the Margaret Bridge and the Árpád Bridge, Margaret Island is popular primarily due its green open areas and tranquillity, its gardens, the Palatinus thermal baths, and the ancient charm of the historical ruins it holds. Five hundred meters wide and about 2.5 kilometers long, motor traffic is prohibited here (the only way to get here is by public bus or taxi), and the island can be crossed only on foot, by bicycle, by carriage or by brin, the characteristic bicycles with two or four seats. Originally formed of three separate little islands, Margit-sziget was known to the Romans, who used the spring waters in the northern part of the island. In medieval times numerous convents were built here. The most important of these was built by the Premostratens order in the 12th century. In the 13th century Béla IV ordered the construction of a Dominican monastery, where, due to a vow by her father, Margaret, one of the king's daughters, was sent to live, and for whom the island was later named in the late 19th century. After the Turkish occupation, almost all the buildings on the island were destroyed, and the island was abandoned. In 1869 the island, which in the meanwhile had been embellished by the gardens ordered by Palatine, was opened to the public, and in 1908 it became city property. To the south is the monument to the Unification, created upon occasion of the hundred year anniversary of the unification of Óbuda, Buda and Pest. Farther north is the athletic complex with the Olympic-sized swimming pool built in 1930-31 by Alfred Hajós, the winner of two gold medals at the 1896 Olympics. A short distance away, the old ruins of the 13th century Franciscan church precede those of the Dominican church and monastery where Margaret lived and the Premostratens church, built in the 11th century, destroyed by the Turks and rebuilt in 1930.

The Riverside Promenade

While the most spectacular view of the city, the river and the surrounding area from the hilly Buda side is certainly from the Royal Palace hill and Mount Gellért, on the Pest side the Dunakorzó, or Danube riverside promenade, which runs from Elizabeth Bridge to the Bridge of Chains, beyond doubt offers the most fascinating and unforgettable views of the capital. Closed to automobile traffic, the avenue is a magical part of Budapest, offering visitors the opportunity to sit on one of the many benches and simply spend a little time watching, abandoning oneself to the pleasure of observing the architectural beauties of the city and the colorful promenade. Far from the more or less obligatory visitors' tours, the noise of the streets and the incessant coming and going of tourists, one can stop and be enchanted by the placid boats crossing the Danube, the antique charm of the Buda shore, where the Citadel of Mount Gellért rises, crowned by the Statue of Liberty, the Royal Palace, the unmistakable form of the Fisherman's Bastion, and Matthias church. All around and to one's back is the teeming Pest, a fabulous view by night as it glitters in the dark sky illuminated by thousands of lights that seem reflected by its majestic 19th century buildings.

Views of the Danube and characteristic details

Index

© and printing: KINA ITALIA / Eurografica - Italy
Text: by Claudia Converso
Design: by Renzo Matino - Schio
Translation: A.B.A. - Milano

Distributed by:
EUROPE UNLIMITED - Budapest
Tel. (1) 430.1877